THE PRITTLEWELL PRINCE
THE DISCOVERY OF A RICH
ANGLO-SAXON BURIAL IN ESSEX

First published in 2004 by
Museum of London Archaeology Service
46 Eagle Wharf Road, London N1 7ED
© Museum of London, 2004

ISBN 1-901992-52-7

Written, designed and photographed by the Museum of London Archaeology Service
Text: Sue Hirst with Taryn Nixon, Peter Rowsome and Susan Wright
Design and production: Tracy Wellman
Photography and reprographics: Andy Chopping and Maggie Cox
Illustrations: Sophie Lamb and Faith Vardy

ACKNOWLEDGEMENTS
The excavations in 2003 at Priory Crescent, Prittlewell, were commissioned and financed by Southend-on-Sea Borough Council. Ian Blair supervised the excavation for MoLAS; Dave Lakin is project manager, Liz Barham conservator and Lyn Blackmore finds specialist. Information on the excavation and finds was provided by the project team.

   MoLAS is very grateful to colleagues at Atkins, Atkins Heritage, the British Museum, English Heritage and the Institute of Archaeology and to many other Anglo-Saxon specialists for help in the study of the Prittlewell finds. The support of English Heritage in providing funds to stabilise and investigate the finds from this internationally important discovery has been crucial.

IMAGES AND PHOTOGRAPHIC CREDITS
Southend Museum Service page 12; The Trustees of the British Museum page 18; National Trust Photographic Library/Joe Cornish page 20; National Trust Photographic Library/Andreas von Einsiedel page 36; all other images are by MoLAS.

CONTENTS

Foreword

Southend-on-Sea, today the largest town in Essex, has a rich and diverse history. Its origins date from long before South End became a seaside resort in the early 19th century. Prittlewell was the medieval village from which Southend-on-Sea grew. But its origins go much further back with evidence for settlement in Anglo-Saxon, Roman and prehistoric times.

The spectacular Anglo-Saxon burial that has now been found adds a new chapter to this fascinating history. David Miles, Chief Archaeologist at English Heritage, has said 'This is a discovery of international importance which stunningly illuminates the rich and complex world of the so-called Dark Ages.' It is hard for today's residents of Southend-on-Sea to believe that this amazing burial and its treasures had been lying, unknown and untouched for over a thousand years, in the shrubbery between busy Priory Crescent and the railway line near Priory Park.

The heritage of the local community and the country as a whole has been enriched by the discovery and Southend-on-Sea Borough Council is delighted to be able to support the study of this splendid find.

Councillor Tony North, Executive Councillor for Leisure, Culture and Sport – Southend-on-Sea Borough Council

OPPOSITE
Archaeologists at work on the body area (left) and the iron weapons (right)

Introduction

In October 2003 the Museum of London Archaeology Service (MoLAS) began an archaeological investigation at Prittlewell in south-east Essex. The work was part of a proposed road improvement on the site of a known Anglo-Saxon cemetery. Within a short time the archaeologists had discovered a burial that was clearly extraordinary. The size of the grave and the quality and quantity of the objects buried there, left little doubt that this was a rare example of a princely burial of the 7th century AD. The fact that the grave was previously undisturbed made it even more significant. It is arguably the most important Anglo-Saxon burial found since the 1939 discovery of the great ship burial at Sutton Hoo in Suffolk.

OPPOSITE
Excavation work in the shrubbery (background) with the burial chamber just beginning to appear in the centre and an Iron Age ditch visible in the left foreground

Bernicia

Rheged

Deira

Elmet

Lindsey

Gwynedd

Mercia

Powys

Middle
Anglia

East
Anglia

Magonsaete

Sutton
Hoo ●

Dyfed

Hwicce

Essex

Southend ●

London ●

Wessex

Kent

Sussex

Dumnonia

0   100km

EARLY SAXON ENGLAND

During the 5th century, after the withdrawal of Roman imperial government, new land-hungry pagan peoples began to arrive in Britain. Angles, Saxons and Jutes – from the Continental coastlands of Holland, northern Germany and Denmark – gained political control of eastern England. The existing inhabitants, some already Christian, were either absorbed into this new Anglo-Saxon society or retreated westwards.

By the late 6th and early 7th century, small 'kingdoms' had formed; the names Sussex (the South Saxons), Essex (East Saxons) and East Anglia (East Angles) preserve their memory. Prittlewell was in the East Saxon kingdom, which was never as rich or as powerful as some of the others, but at one time stretched far beyond modern Essex to include Middlesex and London, south-east Hertfordshire and Surrey.

Kingship was a sign of an increasingly complex society. The greatest warriors and the earliest kings displayed their power through richly decorated clothing, fine weaponry and tableware, gift giving and feasting. Their most valuable possessions were often buried with them. Christian missionaries were sent from Rome to convert these pagan English rulers; religion was highly political.

OPPOSITE
Southern Britain in about AD 600 showing the seven major Saxon kingdoms of East Anglia, Essex, Kent, Mercia, Northumbria (Deira and Bernicia) and Wessex

THE PRITTLEWELL
ANGLO-SAXON CEMETERY

Prittlewell lies on the south-east side of a shallow valley, where the Prittle brook bends to flow north into the River Roach. This pleasant valley attracted settlers in the prehistoric, Roman and Early Saxon periods: it offered water, fertile land and shelter from the exposed Thames estuary to the south. A medieval church, which includes a remnant of an earlier 7th-century Saxon church, survives today. To the north of the church, the grounds of an early 12th-century Cluniac priory (Prittlewell Priory, now parkland) straddled the Prittle brook.

Along the Thames estuary about 2km (1.25 miles) to the south, the hamlet of South End (of Prittlewell) grew up around a break in the cliffs, where the low gravel hills of south Essex reach the river. In 1801 South End numbered 51 houses and was already something of a sea-bathing resort. In 1856 the London, Tilbury and Southend Railway was opened and the growth of Southend-on-Sea as a London commuter town began. The construction of the Great Eastern Railway line in 1887 allowed a northward expansion of Southend and cut through an Anglo-Saxon cemetery at Prittlewell.

ABOVE
Location of the
Prittlewell site

OPPOSITE
The tiny gold foil
crosses found in the
burial (enlarged)

In 1923 Anglo-Saxon and a few Roman burials were found during road building in Priory Crescent. The Anglo-Saxon cemetery appears to extend from the railway, across the road and into Priory Park. The evidence from this early work seemed to suggest the presence of a 6th- to 7th-century Anglo-Saxon cemetery. Although there were at least three graves with female jewellery, there were 19 graves with weapons, including six swords – a striking preponderance of male warrior graves.

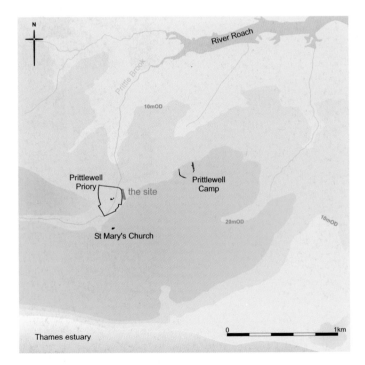

DISCOVERY

It was no surprise then, when in late October 2003 archaeologists working at the site identified three probably Anglo-Saxon graves. One was a classic male warrior burial with a poorly preserved iron sword and knife, and the iron parts – the spearhead and boss – of a spear and shield. What could not have been foreseen was that the excavation would also reveal one of the richest Anglo-Saxon graves ever found.

The first hints, in a trench at the higher, south end of the site, were only faint dark marks in the yellow sand along the edges of what appeared to be an unusually large vertical-sided square pit. As the archaeologists began to empty the pit, they uncovered a large copper-alloy bowl lying on its side in the north-west corner.

This 'hanging bowl', decorated with inlaid enamelled mounts and cruciform strips on its underside, was a rare and beautifully made object. Curiously, one of the suspension rings was hooked over a corroded piece of iron. It became clear that the bowl was still hanging from an iron hook attached to what was once a wall made of upright wooden planks.

As the pit was excavated further, more beautiful vessels

OPPOSITE
Delicate excavation of
the golden rim mounts
from two wooden
drinking vessels

and other metal objects emerged. It became clear that the pit contained a deep, timber-walled underground room, full of objects made of copper alloy, gold, silver and iron: a burial chamber of the highest status, a princely burial indeed. Astonishingly many of the objects were still exactly where they had been placed nearly 1400 years ago, as though frozen in time.

By the end of the excavation more than 100 objects had been removed from the grave, many still embedded in soil blocks, which are being carefully excavated in the conservation laboratory at the Museum of London. Exploration and conservation of the finds and scholarly

BELOW
The copper-alloy
'Coptic' bowl, found
hanging from a hook on
the wall of the burial
chamber

research will continue for several years. The Prittlewell discovery is already benefiting from the use of the latest archaeological methods, both on site and in the laboratory, to teach us more about Anglo-Saxon life than we ever thought possible.

ABOVE
Conservator Liz Barham working on the copper-alloy hanging bowl

17

WHAT IS A PRINCELY BURIAL?

In the late 6th and early 7th centuries burial mounds or barrows began to be built over a wide area of England. Some of these barrow burials were large and complex structures containing a wealth of objects. They have been interpreted, like similar burials in Europe and Scandinavia, as the resting places of members of leading aristocratic and royal families – warrior princes and their families flaunting their wealth and power.

In England princely burials are found beneath mounds of 10–20 metres in diameter, often situated in prominent positions commanding long views. Some were cremation burials; in other cases the body was buried intact (inhumed) as at Prittlewell – Benty Grange (Derbyshire), Broomfield (Essex), Caenby (Lincolnshire), Cuddesdon (Oxfordshire), Sutton Hoo mounds 1, 2, and 17 (Suffolk), and Taplow (Buckinghamshire). The Broomfield barrow burial (just north of Chelmsford) is the only other princely burial in Essex of similar date and comparable status to the Prittlewell chamber grave. Most such barrow burials had been looted

OPPOSITE
The 1882 excavation of the princely burial at Taplow, Buckinghamshire

hundreds of years ago, or dug by 19th-century antiquarians. Of the inhumation burials, only Sutton Hoo mounds 1 and 17, and now Prittlewell, were previously undisturbed and excavated under modern excavation conditions.

The inhumations were sometimes housed in burial chambers, occasionally, as at Sutton Hoo, in or below ships. The majority are male but there are some females – both typically found with exotic imported objects and/or Anglo-Saxon versions of such objects. The male burials often

include clothing accessories such as buckles, sets of weapons and other objects celebrating the male warrior, for example jewelled swords, ornamented shields and helmets. There are also lyres (stringed musical instruments), gaming pieces (rather like chequers counters) and equipment for eating and especially for drinking, such as cauldrons, buckets, bowls, glass jars, drinking horns, cups and beakers. The finds conjure up a splendid society that celebrated with feasting and ceremony. In *Beowulf*, one of the earliest poems in the English language, there is a vivid description of feasting in the great hall called Heorot.

Then a bench was cleared in that banquet hall
so the Geats could have room to be together
and the party sat, proud in their bearing,
strong and stalwart. An attendant stood by
with a decorated pitcher, pouring bright
helpings of mead. And the minstrel sang
filling Heorot with his head-clearing voice

(*BEOWULF*, LINES 491–7
TRANSLATION BY SEAMUS HEANEY)

THE BURIAL CHAMBER

The Prittlewell burial chamber was 4 metres (13 feet) square, with a timber-planked floor and walls set in a pit 1.4 metres (nearly 5 feet) deep. Along the north side of this underground wooden room, a body was laid in or on a wooden structure with iron fittings; this may have been a coffin or a more complex structure such as a bed. Bone preservation in sandy soils is often very poor and no trace of human bone was found but two copper-alloy shoe buckles tell us that the body had been laid with its feet to the east. This was confirmed in the laboratory, when fragments of human tooth enamel were found in a soil sample from the head end of the burial. The presence of weapons and absence of female jewellery makes it almost certain that this was the burial of a man.

OPPOSITE
A reconstruction of the Prittlewell burial chamber by Faith Vardy, showing the arrangement of grave goods as found

LEFT
An X-ray image of the shoe buckles and possible buckle plates within a soil block lifted from the burial chamber

OPPOSITE
(From top left) glass
jars, wooden drinking
vessels with decorative
metal rim mounts and
a drinking horn found
along the east wall of
the burial chamber

It is clear from the astonishing array of grave goods laid out around the body and on the walls of the chamber that this was a man of high status. Just looking into the excavated chamber gave an unforgettable impression of the splendid and dramatic burial, which had been arranged by and for the mourners of a great man.

When the funeral ceremony was over, a wooden cover was placed over the body and a plank roof laid across the chamber. Finally a barrow (a mound of earth) about 10 metres (33 feet) across was raised above it. In time the plank roof began to collapse and sandy soil filtered into the open chamber preserving the objects in their original positions. Whatever remained of the mound was probably ploughed away in the medieval period and all knowledge of the burial was lost – until now.

RIGHT
The ornate copper-alloy
and gold mounts on the
rim of a drinking horn

24

THE GRAVE GOODS

The grave goods – the objects buried in the grave – include dress fittings, personal equipment and possessions, weapons and regalia, and vessels of many kinds, together with objects suggesting recreation. There were probably many items of textile and other organic materials present, and we may find traces of these during the laboratory work.

Dress fittings and personal equipment

The pristine gold belt buckle has a hollow triangular buckle plate with three rivets with decorative boss mounts on the front face. This form of buckle is a Continental style that was also copied in Kent. It could have been imported but was probably made in England. The fashion was most popular about AD 600–640. This is only the third example of a gold buckle from an early Anglo-Saxon burial in England.

The small copper-alloy shoe buckles are of a standard form and are virtually identical to those found in the Sutton Hoo mound 1 burial.

Minute traces of gold braid found in the chest area may have ornamented the edge of a garment, such as the neck of a tunic. Two gold coins, both tremisses from Merovingian

ABOVE
An X-ray image of the gold braid

OPPOSITE
A rare and beautiful gold belt buckle from the burial (enlarged)

France, were found, one above and one below the waist. The first, thought to be of the moneyer Ioannes (John) of Cadolidi or Capolidi (location uncertain), probably dates to the early 7th century. The front shows a very crude diademed bust; the back an unusual cross. The inscription on the front of the second coin tells us that it was issued in Paris, while the back gives the name of the moneyer, Vitalis. This coin belongs to a series that was in use from about AD 570/580 to 670. Another gold coin of the same type is a chance find from Southend.

Two tiny gold-foil Latin crosses were found in the head area and are undoubtedly Christian symbols. They are a unique find for Britain but are found in Continental burials in Lombardic Italy and in Alamannia (south-west Germany and northern Switzerland) in the late 6th and 7th centuries. Their presence at Prittlewell suggests connections with Italy – there is historical evidence for Roman missionary activity in late 6th- and early 7th-century south-east England. Such crosses are thought to have been custom-made for burial. They may have been attached to clothing or to a veil placed over the face and may symbolise allegiance to the Christian church of Rome.

Other personal possessions were found in the remains of a small, possibly painted, wooden box in the south-west corner of the burial chamber. Items in the box included a small copper-alloy cylinder with a lid and a silver Byzantine spoon, probably made in the 6th century. A two-line Latin inscription, illegible apart from the letters 'FAB...' and possibly 'RONAM', may have been added in the 7th century. The cross above the lettering may be Christian, although inscriptions of this date often start with a cross.

Weapons and other symbols of power

An iron sword and iron fittings from a (now decayed) wooden shield were found on the floor on the south side of the chamber and a further large iron object may be another weapon. Much more work is needed to understand these objects but an X-ray of the sword shows the handle end with two serrated ring fittings, possibly in gold. There are also buckle-like shapes in the soil block, which may be part of a sword belt.

Two other iron objects are much more unusual and suggest the very high status of the dead man. An iron stand about 1.33 metres (over 4 feet) high was found still upright on its four feet in the north-east corner of the chamber. X-rays show that the base was made of four curved strips, welded together at the shaft. The shaft itself is twisted at intervals for decorative effect; it tapers to a point and has at least two additional side prongs. The Prittlewell stand may have been a royal standard, perhaps holding a banner, or a stand to hold a burning wooden torch or candles.

At the head end of the burial, against the west wall of the chamber, was an iron folding stool, the first to be found in an Anglo-Saxon grave. Similar stools are represented in early medieval images of kings and emperors, and other Continental examples come from high-status graves. Detailed examination of the Prittlewell stool, which at the time of writing is still in its dense soil block, may reveal decorative inlays.

BELOW
Excavating the iron frame of the folding stool

Vessels

So far some 22 vessels have been identified, a number only exceeded by the 43 vessels from the Sutton Hoo mound 1 burial.

Vessels hanging from the walls

Four copper-alloy vessels were found hanging on iron hooks on the chamber wall. They include the hanging bowl and a Byzantine flagon on the north wall, and a large 'Coptic' copper-alloy bowl and a copper-alloy cauldron with iron handle on the east wall.

Bronze hanging bowls have been found in other graves in England but complete examples from well-dated contexts are rare. The decorative strips on the outside of this bowl stand proud of the body and lead to decorated circular mounts to which the four suspension rings attached to the rim are fastened. The circular mount on the inside of the base has red enamel decoration. The design appears to incorporate two geometric birds/beasts and a floral motif. No exact parallel for this hanging bowl is known. It was probably made in Ireland or the north of England in the 6th century or 7th century.

The flagon was cast in a mould, shouldered with a slightly convex base and a lid that is secured to the ornate handle by means of a chain. The handle was made separately and is attached to the neck by a plain band and to the body by a second band, the central part of which has three embossed medallions of figures, possibly saints, on horses facing to the left. Vessels of this type were made in the eastern

Mediterranean between the 6th and 9th centuries. They were widely exported but this is the first example found in an archaeological context in England.

The plain 'Coptic' bowl with its foot ring and two hinged handles comes from the same general eastern Mediterranean source as the flagon but is less rare. The main distribution of such bowls in England is in East Anglia and Kent, where they can be dated to the first half of the 7th century.

The small cauldron has a rounded body and perforated upstanding triangular lugs into which the iron handle was slotted. It is possible that this piece was old when buried, as most of the examples found in Anglo-Saxon graves date to the 6th century.

Drinking cups and jars

Ranged along the floor of the chamber against the east wall, immediately to the south of the feet of the body, was an array of wooden and horn drinking vessels and two matching pairs of glass jars.

The blue glass squat jars are decorated with an applied floral design of seven petals on the base and plaitwork of three overlapping wavy lines around the body. The smaller green glass squat jars have one trail that creates five petals around the base/lower body and another spiral trail round the neck. These glass vessels and some similar ones from Essex and especially Kent were probably all made by the same craftsman, probably in Kent, in AD 580–630, although most

English finds of squat jars seem to be from 7th-century contexts.

The drinking vessels include the remains of five wooden cups with gilded copper-alloy or silver rim mounts decorated with interlace ornament in the Scandinavian style. Another two cups were found on the north side of the chamber. These cups were almost certainly made in England and similar vessels have been found in other high-status burials, often made of maplewood.

Two drinking horns were also found, although only the fittings and horn rim survived. On one a broad gilded copper-alloy band around the rim of the horn is decorated with a beaded interlace pattern. This band was held in place by a

separate curved strip that protects the rim and by a lower band that also secured the 12 gold-foil triangular mounts. The last elements to be applied were the three vertical mounts with animal heads that hook over the rim and are riveted to the lower strip. The decorative style of the metalwork can be dated to the 7th century. Drinking horns are extremely rare and are only found in graves of the highest status. Literary sources tell us that the horn was probably from an auroch (a large wild ox, now extinct) rather than domestic cattle.

Every-day vessels

The remaining vessels in the chamber are more utilitarian. An enormous copper-alloy cauldron was placed on its side so

that it would fit between the foot of the burial and the chamber wall. It would probably have had a chain for suspension.

Two medium-sized iron-bound wooden buckets lay in the south-east corner of the chamber, next to the drinking vessels. Anglo-Saxon buckets like these are made of wooden staves fixed to a wooden base and held together with iron bands; they would have been watertight.

In the north-west corner of the burial chamber stood a much bigger iron-bound wooden bucket or tub. It is badly compressed and distorted, but it was probably about 480mm (19in) in diameter and 450mm (18in) tall. If so, it would have contained about 81.5 litres (18 gallons) when full. Attached to the iron binding around the rim are two large rings for suspension or carrying and between these are opposed triangular mounts that would have strengthened the body.

When the fill of the tub was removed in the laboratory two objects were found inside. The first was a small copper-alloy bowl with flanged rim. Marks on the surface suggest it was shaped on a lathe. In the bottom of the bucket was a large straight iron scythe blade with right-angled handle attachment. The scythe would have had a long handle and is a rare find, the few other similar examples being later Saxon. Perhaps the tub, the scythe and the bowl were associated with grain and symbolise the role of the buried man as food provider.

ABOVE
A small copper-alloy bowl found inside the wooden tub

BELOW
Reconstructed iron-bound tub from Sutton Hoo

Entertainment

Two objects found in the chamber represent the sort of entertainment provided in the feasting hall – board games and music.

The 57 plain bone gaming pieces were found between the foot end of the burial and the north wall of the chamber, and were probably buried in a bag. Saxon gaming pieces are typically of domed form like these and were probably made of slices from the ball heads of the upper leg bones of cattle. The Prittlewell set is remarkable both for the number of pieces and the fact that they are associated with two extremely large dice made from antler.

BELOW
Some of the bone
gaming pieces

Towards the east end of the south side of the chamber was a musical instrument. A dark patch on the floor of the chamber turned out to be the complete outline of a wooden lyre with gilded copper-alloy, silver and iron fittings, some perhaps repairs. Other excavated examples suggest that the lyre would have had six strings, probably of gut, and a wrist strap. It may have been buried in a bag or case. Lyres were very important to the Anglo-Saxons and their Continental neighbours, providing the essential musical accompaniment to their heroic verse.

WHO WAS THE PRITTLEWELL PRINCE?

The objects in the grave tell us that this was the burial of a man of high rank but there is nothing so far which can help us to identify a named individual. Nor can we say what the Prittlewell prince looked like – how tall he was, whether he was young or old – because his bones did not survive, not even a shadow.

The artefacts from the Prittlewell burial, of types well dated across Europe and the eastern Mediterranean, suggest that burial took place between about AD 600 and 650. It may be possible to refine this dating as study continues. The grave goods represent great wealth but fall short of the largesse buried in Sutton Hoo mound 1 with its gold and garnet dress fittings and ornate gold purse containing 37 gold coins.

The presence of 'foreign' objects in the Prittlewell grave does not necessarily suggest direct or continuous trade links between these countries and the East Saxon kingdom – many of the items could have been received as individual gifts. Other objects suggest a strong connection with Kent,

OPPOSITE
Excavation supervisor
Ian Blair carefully
revealing the gold
buckle

perhaps some of the gifts came from his powerful neighbours across the Thames.

The Prittlewell burial is second only to the Sutton Hoo mound 1 burial in riches, but it differs from the other known princely burials in being placed apparently within or on the edge of a contemporary Anglo-Saxon cemetery – it is not an isolated barrow or part of a separate elite barrow cemetery like Sutton Hoo. Nor does it command a long view but one along the Prittle valley northwards to the Roach estuary.

Although the manner of the burial – a chamber grave beneath a barrow mound with many grave goods – is that of a very high-status pagan, some of the grave goods suggest contact with Christianity. The Coptic bowl and flagon, with medallions of a possible saint, might have been used for the

BELOW
The inscribed bowl of the silver spoon; the lettering is clearest to the left, with the cross in the top centre

ritual washing of hands or feet; the silver spoon may have been a baptismal gift, to be used in taking communion. More particularly the presence of the gold-foil crosses on the body and the relative simplicity of the man's dress fittings and personal equipment suggest that he was a Christian at his death.

If we look to history to identify a Christian king of the East Saxons in the first half of the 7th century, with strong connections with Kent, then Sabert is the only obvious candidate. Bede, writing his history in the early 8th century, tells how Ethelbert of Kent, who governed all the English peoples as far north as the Humber in the late 6th and early 7th centuries and whose wife was a Frankish Christian princess, was converted to Christianity by Augustine in AD 597. In 604, Augustine, archbishop of Britain, appointed Bishop Mellitus 'to preach in the province of the East Saxons, which is separated from Kent by the River Thames and bounded on the east by the sea. Its capital is the city of London, which stands on the banks of the Thames, and is a trading centre for many nations who visit it by land and sea. At this time Sabert, Ethelbert's nephew through his sister Ricula, ruled the province under the suzerainty of Ethelbert. When this province too had received the faith ... King Ethelbert built a church dedicated to the holy Apostle Paul in the city of London, which he appointed as the episcopal see of Mellitus and his successors.'

Ethelbert of Kent died in 616 and was buried in his church

ABOVE
Embossed medallion
from the flagon,
showing a horse-
mounted figure,
possibly a saint

in Canterbury where Bertha his queen also lay. Sabert died in the same year but Bede does not say that he was buried in the church at London. He writes that when Sabert 'departed for the heavenly kingdom he left three sons, all pagans, to inherit his earthly kingdom. These were quick to profess idolatry, which they had pretended to abandon during the lifetime of their father, and encouraged their people to return to the old gods'; Bishop Mellitus was banished. It was not until AD 653 that Sabert's grandson, Sigebert 'Sanctus', was persuaded to adopt Christianity by Northumbrian missionaries under Saint Cedd.

Sigebert is probably too late for our man and it is tempting to suggest that the Prittlewell burial is that of the Christian East Saxon king, Sabert, defiantly buried by his sons in pagan splendour, rather than in the church at London.

If the Prittlewell burial is that of a Saxon king, why is he not as richly attired and equipped as his contemporary in Sutton Hoo mound 1? Perhaps his relatively modest dress reflects his Christian faith. It is also possible that the king buried in Sutton Hoo mound 1 was Raedwald, who was the first high king of all England, while the 'Prittlewell prince' may have been a king of the East Saxons alone.

OPPOSITE
The burial chamber viewed from the south-west, showing grave goods in place (digital photomontage)